Black Reverence

GRAPHIC POETRY IN LOVE'S FULL COLOR

Sefa Noir

Andrea Johnson Books Publishing

Black Reverence

© 2020 Sefa Noir. All rights reserved

Cover art designed by Andrea Johnson Books Publishing

No part of this book may be reproduced, stored in a retrieval system, or transmitted by any means without the written permission of the author.

First published by Andrea Johnson Books Publishing. 05/27/2020

6565 N. MacArthur Blvd, Suite 225 Dallas, TX. 75039 www.Ajbpublishing.com

This book is a work of fiction. Names, characters, places, and incidents are the product of the author's imagination or are used fictitiously. Any resemblance to actual events, locales, or persons, living or dead, is coincidental.

Because of the dynamic nature of the Internet, any web addresses or links contained in this book may have changed since publication and may no longer be valid. The views expressed in this work are solely those of the author and do not necessarily reflect the views of the publisher, and the publisher herby disclaims any responsibility for them.

ISBN: 978-0-578-67629-6

Introduction

You seduced me with one sentence and the falling rain and moonlight became the backdrop of our passion. We were taken hostage by our own impulsive desires and had no care to be free again. Your intensity pulled me in like the moon moves the ocean. Your darkness and power became an insatiable craving and I awoke after each encounter wanting more. It was the fullness of your lips, energy of your being, and the blackness of a people that stretches back before recorded time emerging from your words, and I do nothing less but give myself as a gift in reverence.

Sefa Noir

It was the sweetness

Of your cocoa brown kisses

Black Reverence

Amid all the noise, the only sound that matters is when you whisper my name.

You brought my heart in out of the cold, and warmed it by your fire.

Black Reverence

I fell into the depths of your ebony skin and wanted to drown.

Sefa Noir

Black Reverence

It was the brightness of your smile that captured me,

And the passion of your touch that enslaved me.

Sefa Noir

You breathed life into my dreams,

And depth into my every fantasy.

In my soul, his name was Zahir, for he was the manifestation of all I had asked for.

Sefa Noir

The insanity of our passion

Has kept me sane

Black Reverence

The sweet taste of your skin on my tongue, became the addiction I refused to give up.

Sefa Noir

And you saw my soul...

No other words
Were needed.

Black Reverence

I love not knowing where you end...
and I begin.

Black Reverence

It was always you my flesh and soul cried out for.

Sefa Noir

Missing you was Not an option,

Needing you Became a Necessity.

Black Reverence

You are enough...more than enough, and I will savor every bite of you.

Sefa Noir

You are the water soft enough to cleanse me,

The ocean deep enough To drown me.

The storm strong enough to Save me.

Black Reverence

Quickly you became the compass towards my every happiness.

Sefa Noir

There was never a day

When you Were not Mine.

Sefa Noir

The need for your kiss became greater than my darkest addiction.

When we met, the universe whispered "Jahaneman" and I knew I found the soul of me.

Sefa Noir

I needed to warm myself by the fire within you.

Black Reverence

You are the beginning to all my pleasures

And the center

Of all my

Desires.

Sefa Noir

My flesh trembles at the power of your words,

And the caress of your Whisper.

Black Reverence

Black Reverence

Listening to your heartbeat, reminds me that I am alive.

Sefa Noir

I can't get enough of the taste of your brown sugar, honey, and gold.

Black Reverence

Sefa Noir

Black Reverence

Sefa Noir

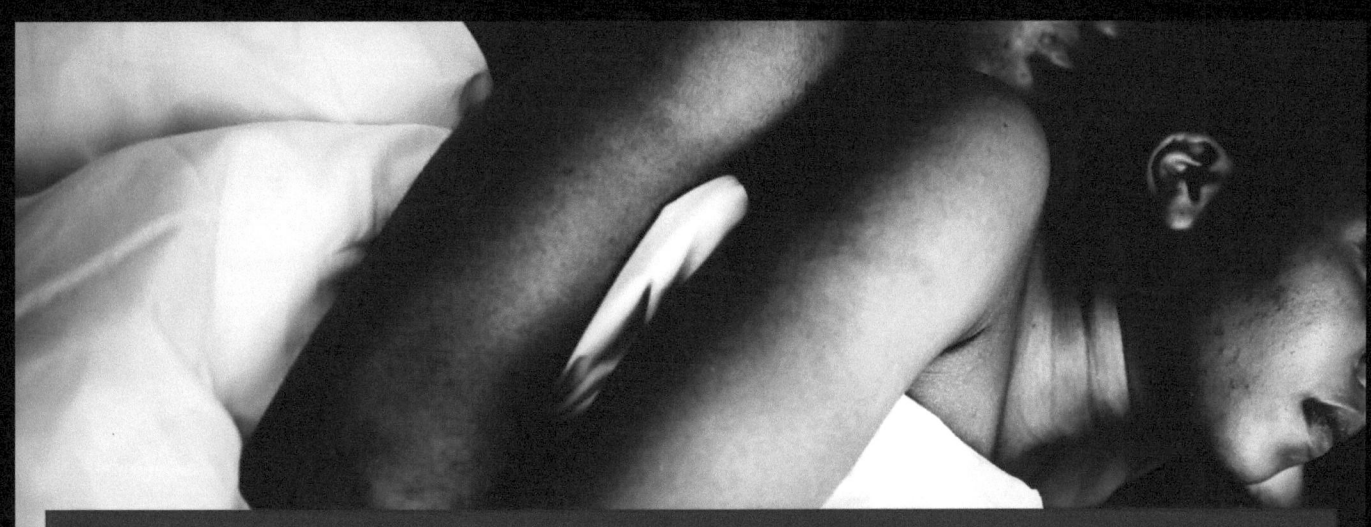

ABOUT THE AUTHOR

Sefa Noir's corporate life is a focused executive HR professional, who mentors' employees on careers and their dreams.

When not working as an executive, she writes poetry to record her thoughts, feelings, beliefs and dreams about the human condition, relationships, and love.

To learn more about Sefa Noir and her upcoming soulful works of poetry, visit her profile on

The publishing website:

www.AJBPublishing.com or follow her on Instagram @Sefa_Noir

www.ingramcontent.com/pod-product-compliance
Lightning Source LLC
Chambersburg PA
CBHW040356190426
43201CB00039B/35